HANS OF ICELAND

Borgo Press Books by VICTOR HUGO

Hans of Iceland: A Play in Three Acts (with Palmir, Octo, and Rameau)
Les Misérables: A Play in Two Acts (with Paul Meurice & Charles Victor Hugo)
Ninety-Three: A Play in Four Acts (with Paul Meurice)

HANS OF ICELAND

A PLAY IN THREE ACTS

PALMIR, OCTO, &

RAMEAU

Adapted from the Story by Victor Hugo
Translated by Frank J. Morlock

THE BORGO PRESS
MMXIII

HANS OF ICELAND

Copyright © 2001, 2013 by Frank J. Morlock

FIRST BORGO PRESS EDITION

Published by Wildside Press LLC

www.wildsidebooks.com

DEDICATION

To my friend Victor Lantang

CONTENTS

CAST OF CHARACTERS. 9
ACT I, Scene 1 11
ACT I, Scene 2 23
ACT I, Scene 3 41
ACT II, Scene 4. 57
ACT II, Scene 5. 67
ACT III, Scene 6 89
ACT III, Scene 7 101
ACT III, Scene 8 113
ACT III, Scene 9 125
ABOUT THE AUTHOR 139

CAST OF CHARACTERS

HANS OF ICELAND, outlaw

ORDENER GULDENLEN, son of the Viceroy of Norway

COUNT D'ALEFELD, Chancellor of Denmark and Norway

COUNT HARALD, former Chancellor

FREDERIC, a young officer, son of Count D'Alefeld

SPIAGURDY, guardian of Drontheim

KENNIBOL, Young Musketeer of Munckholm

ORUGIX, The Executioner

TIRCLA, Concierge of the prison

OGLIPIGLAP, Lapplander, assistant to Spiagudry

A SYNDIC

AN OFFICER

ESILDA, Harald's daughter

BECHLIE, wife of Orugix

OLLY, Old Matron of Drontheim

MAASE, another Matron of Drontheim

A VILLAGER

A YOUNG VILLAGE GIRL

NORWEGIANS

MUSKETEERS FROM MUNCKOLM

ACT I
SCENE 1

The action takes place in Drontheim in Norway.

The stage represents a hall made completely of stone. Through a door in the rear can be seen a public square. Midstage, to the left is a grill with a small gate, above which reads: Room of the Dead.

AT RISE, several of the people are occupied looking through the bars of the grill. Notable among them are Kennibol, Maase and Olly. Spiagudry, seated on a stool at the right seems to be asleep.

OLLY:

Now that's where love gets you, neighbor Maase. That poor Gath wouldn't be there stretched on that black stone if she had only thought of patching the nets of her unfortunate father.

MAASE:

And her fiancée, Gill Stadt, that handsome young man that you see beside her wouldn't be there, if, instead of making love to Gath, and seeking his fortune in the accursed mines of Roras where he was crushed by falling rocks, he had remained by his infirm mother who now weeps before the empty cradle of her child, grown into a big young man—and dead.

OLLY:

Gath drowned herself in despair at the death of her fiancée?

KENNIBOL:

Who said that? This girl, who I knew quite well, was indeed the fiancée of this young miner, but she was also the mistress of one of my comrades, a soldier from the garrison of Munckolm; and the day before yesterday she wanted to get into the fortress by stealth in order to celebrate with her lover the death of her betrothed. The boat that was carrying her capsized on a reef and she drowned.

OLLY:

How horrible! How can one take delight in spreading such absurdities?

MAASE:

It's an infamous slander.

SPIAGUDRY:

(waking up)

Silence, driveling old witches.

OLLY:

Heavens, you hear him, the damned old soul?

MAASE:

What's he want of us? This big cadaver who guards cadavers.

SPIAGUDRY:

Peace I tell you, daughters of Hell. If today is the Sabbath, hurry to take up your brooms; otherwise, they will fly off without you. (to Kenniobl) You were saying, my brave man, that this wretched woman?

OLLY:

The old wise guy! We are wretched women because our bodies, if they fall into his hands, bring him nothing besides the tax. Only thirty escalins, while he would receive forty for the miserable carcass of a man.

SPIAGUDRY:

Will you viper tongues quiet down! Tell me, my brave man, your comrade whose mistress was this Gath, doubtless killed himself in despair at having lost her?

MAASE:

Do you hear this old pagan? He would see one less among the living because of the forty escalins a dead body would bring him.

SPIAGUDRY:

Come on, don't get angry, my sweet gossips. Mustn't everyone in the world live by his profession?

KENNIBOL:

Well, old Satan, where do you intend to get with this friendly grimace that resembles so nicely the last outburst of laughter of a hanged man?

SPIAGUDRY:

Here I am. When the bodies they bring us have been found in the water, we are obliged to share half the reward with the fishermen. Therefore, my valiant friend, I would pray you to engage your unfortunate comrade not to drown himself but to choose some other type of death; the thing must be indifferent to him, he ought not to work harm, as he does to the unfortunate Christians who will give hospitality to his body if the loss of Gath pushes him to this act of despair.

KENNIBOL:

That's where you are mistaken, my charitable and hospitable concierge of the dead. My comrade would have no satisfaction to be received in your appetizing inn, for at the moment he's consoling himself with another beauty for the death of this one.

OLLY:

What is the wretch saying now?

MAASE:

You love rogues like this?

SPIAGUDRY:

Peace! One more time. Truly, the torture of Beelzebub is really frightful if he is required to hear such choirs if only once a week.

(uproar and rage of the women)

OGLIPIGLAP:

(entering)

Master Spiagudry, I announce a new pensioner to you.

SPIAGUDRY:

Marvelous! Where's he coming from?

OGLIPIGLAP:

From the beaches of Urchtal.

SPIAGUDRY:

Fine! Fine! (rubbing his hands) Have him brought in through the small gate.

(goes out with his assistant.)

MAASE:

Doubtless it's another victim of love or ambition.

KENNIBOL:

(looking through the bars of the grill)

By my saber! It's an officer of my regiment. He appears to be a suicide.

OLLY:

Say rather he's been murdered for he was found on the beach of Urchtal and it's known Hans of Iceland wanders on those beaches.

MAASE:

Yes. And what's more no one is unaware that the Icelander murders in a manner so diabolical that his victims are often taken for suicides.

KENNIBOL:

What sort of man is this Hans?

OLLY:

He's a giant.

MAASE:

No. He's a dwarf.

KENNIBOL:

No one's seen him?

MAASE:

Those who see him for the first time see him for the last as well.

OLLY:

(mysteriously)

Hush! They say there are only three people who have ever exchanged human words with him. This reprobate Spiagudry, the widow Stadt and her son, the poor Gill that you see here.

KENNIBOL:

(still looking through the grill)

Oh, now I am certain that it is Captain Dispolsen, who was coming from Copenhagen and who was expected this morning at Munckolm. I recognize the steel chain that our state prisoner, Old Harald, gave him on his departure.

ORDENER:

(coming forward excitedly)

You are sure that this is Captain Dispolsen?

KENNIBOL:

Certain. On the glory of Saint Beelzebub, my patron.

ORDENER:

(leaving)

Poor Count! Unfortunate Harald! One friend remained to you; you've lost him and now only Ordener is interesting himself in you.

(goes out)

SPIAGUDRY:

Come, night is approaching, my old friends: vanish. Enough wagging your tongues, now you must wag your legs.

OLLY:

(mockingly)

Good evening, Doctor Spiagudry.

MAASE:

Good evening, old monopolist of cadavers.

KENNIBOL:

Good evening, neighbor. Carefully close up your morgue for fear someone will come to steal your dead from you.

SPIAGUDRY:

Neighbor? Say rather, your host. For I really hope that one of these days, I will rent you one of my stone beds for a week.

(Spiagudry, having closed the exterior gate, moves

away to the right.)

BLACKOUT/CURTAIN

ACT I
SCENE 2

The stage represents a long, dimly lit gothic gallery. To the left a half-open door.

FREDERIC:

(entering in the brilliant costume of an officer, in a light tone)

This devil of a Captain Dispolsen never arrives. How long does he expect us to wait for him? What's he been doing at Copenhagen? What relations exist between him and our prisoner, the former Chancellor of the Realm, Count Harald? I will discover it. But to reach that goal how many days must I remain enshrouded in this sad dungeon, far from so many beauties who sigh for my return? Filial obedience. How dearly you cost me at this moment.

A SOLDIER:

(entering)

An officer requests to speak to you.

FREDERIC:

An officer? Let him be introduced. Doubtless it's Dispolsen.

(going up to Ordener, who enters)

Greetings, Captain. You didn't suspect that you would be making wait a man who does not have the satisfaction of knowing you. By my word, I won't be able to congratulate you on your return to this lugubrious castle. As for me, I am horribly bored by it. And but for my father's orders, for I have to tell you Captain, that my father is the present Chancellor who has ordered me—You understand me, with respect to the daughter of the prisoner.

But I am wasting all my efforts. This pretty statue is not a woman; she's always weeping and pays no attention to me.

ORDENER:

What! Ordered to seduce the daughter of this unfortunate?

FREDERIC:

I would challenge the devil to seduce her. Day before yesterday, being of the guard, expressly for her I wore a delicious French style girdle. Would you believe she didn't even raise her eyes to look at me?

ORDENER:

(striking his own face with indignation)

Is it possible?

FREDERIC:

(somewhat louder)

Not the least attention to me, word of honor. By the way, what new fashions are at the court, Captain Dispolsen?

ORDENER:

(as if awakening)

I am not Captain Dispolsen.

FREDERIC:

(with surprise and in a severe tone)

What? And who are you then to introduce yourself here, at this hour?

ORDENER:

(displaying a parchment)

I wish to see the Grand Chancellor of Norway, your prisoner.

FREDERIC:

Right. This document is in order. Ah, your name is Ordener. By the way, you know, sir, that Ordener, son of the viceroy must directly marry my sister and that consequently—

ORDENER:

Thanks for your family details; I desire to see the prisoner.

FREDERIC:

Hold on; He's coming this way. This room is part of his prison. I will leave you with him.

(aside as he leaves)

Dummy that I am. I really am afraid that I've committed an indiscretion.

HARALD:

(plunged in a deep reverie enters without seeing Ordener; after being seated, he says)

Dispolsen has surely abandoned and betrayed me. Men! Men are like this icicle that an Arab takes for a diamond; he will place it carefully in his haversack and when he looks for it he will find no more than a little water.

ORDENER:

I am not one of those men, Lord Count.

HARALD:

Who's speaking to me? Lord Count? Is it to flatter me

that you call me thus? You're wasting your time, I am no longer powerful.

ORDENER:

The one who speaks to you never knew you powerful and is none the less your friend for all that.

HARALD:

He still hopes for something from me. The memories kept of the wretched always measure themselves to the hopes that remain of them.

ORDENER:

It's I who ought to complain, noble count, for I remember you and you've forgotten me. I am Ordener!

HARALD:

(with joy)

Ordener! Be welcome; a thousand joyous wishes to the traveler who remembers the prisoner!

ORDENER:

Then you were no longer counting on my return, Count

Harald?

HARALD:

The old captive no longer counts on anything. But he has a young daughter who remarked to him this very evening that a year has elapsed since your absence.

ORDENER:

(transported)

Your Esilda, Lord, has deigned to count the moments since my departure!

HARALD:

Use your liberty young man so long as you have joy in it. Tell me, have you still your mad ideas of independence?

ORDENER:

If I didn't have these crazy ideas I wouldn't be here.

HARALD:

And yet you run through the world, you have rank in it, perhaps, for despite your discretion, everything proclaims you to have an elevated birth. Poor fool, independence is only found in retreat, in isolation.

ORDENER:

You don't like men, noble count?

HARALD:

I weep to be a man, and I laugh at the one who seeks to console me. You will learn, if you are still ignorant of it, misfortune breeds defiancé as prosperity breeds ingratitude. But inform me what favorable wind has blown on Captain Dispolsen? Some lucky thing must have happened to him since he forgets me.

ORDENER:

(embarrassed)

Dispolsen, Lord Count? It's to speak to you of him that I came this evening. I know he enjoyed your complete confidence.

HARALD:

Young man, you are mistaken! No being in the world has my confidence. Dispolsen, it's true, has my most important papers. It's for me that he went to Copenhagen to the King.

I will even confess that I counted more on him than on any other. For in my prosperity I had never done him any service.

ORDENER:

Well! Noble Count, I saw him today.

HARALD:

Your trouble tells me the rest; he's a traitor?

ORDENER:

He is dead!

HARALD:

Dead.

(moment of silence)

When I told you that something had happened to him—it's not him I complain of. He's only a man at least; it's not I that have lost! But my daughter, my unfortunate daughter, What will become of her if they take her unfortunate father from her? How did Dispolsen die? Where did you see him?

ORDENER:

I saw him at the morgue; dead, murdered.

HARALD:

Then I know from whence the blow proceeds; all is lost. He was bringing me proofs of a conspiracy they are laying against me. They've known how to destroy them.

Unfortunate, Esilda!

ORDENER:

From the nature of Dispolsen's wounds, they think his assassin is this famous brigand, named Hans of Iceland. He has skinned the captain.

HARALD:

(with anxiety)

You didn't hear of a coffer of iron sealed with the arms of my house?

ORDENER:

No, lord, but each knows that Hans of Iceland to avenge the death of a young miner, that is said to be his son, has sworn the annihilation of all who wear the uniform of the Musketeers of Munckolm. The monster's implacable hate could be the sole cause of the murder.

HARALD:

Poor Esilda! Unhappy coffer!

ORDENER:

I will bring it back to you, Lord. The crime was committed this morning. They say Hans of Iceland has fled to the North. I've often run through the mountains of Drontheimbus. I will extinguish the brigand.

HARALD:

Noble Ordener, goodbye. May you succeed in your enterprise! The happiness of my daughter depends upon it.

(Ordener presses the hand of the old man who moves away)

ORDENER:

(alone)

The Unfortunate! Ah! May he be unaware still of my name! What would he say in learning that I am the son of the Viceroy, of the one who has for so many years unjustly detained him; who today pays for his past services—thirty years of honor and probity—with exile and prison. Oh father, may you know the truth as I do! Fatal condition of kings that a crowd presses about them, avid for honors and wealth, surrounding them with out cease like a cloud that veils the day light. But who is this young girl prostrated before the image of the mother of the savior? It's Esilda. She's rising and coming this way. Happy Ordener! How beautiful she is!

ESILDA:

(entering)

Ah, it's Ordener! It's Lord Ordener.

ORDENER:

It's him, Countess Esilda.

ESILDA:

Why do you call me Countess?

ORDENER:

Why do you call me Lord?

ESILDA:

Doubtless you've been a long while at Drontheim? Your absence from this castle cannot seem long to you.

ORDENER:

Esilda!

ESILDA:

Oh. Don't look at me with that severe eye; have I offended you? Can't you pardon a poor prisoner, you who spend your days with some beautiful and noble lady, free and happy like you?

ORDENER:

Who? Me, Countess?

ESILDA:

Don't speak of me like that; I am no longer Countess to anyone, especially to you.

ORDENER:

Well! My Esilda, my adored Esilda, call me your Ordener. Tell me, do you still love me?

ESILDA:

During your absence, I haven't had any other happiness than the presence of an unfortunate, of my father. I spend my days consoling him and hoping for you.

ORDENER:

Dear Esilda.

ESILDA:

This prison where I've spent all my life until now was becoming odious to me, and yet, before your arrival, my father had always filled it for me. But you were no longer here and I desired this liberty I've never known.

ORDENER:

Well! My Esilda, I no longer want this freedom except you can share it.

ESILDA:

What! Ordener, you won't leave us any more?

ORDENER:

Friend, I must leave you again until such time as I may return never to leave you again.

ESILDA:

Alas! Absent again.

ORDENER:

Esilda, it's a question of your father's life.

ESILDA:

Of my father's life!

ORDENER:

Yes, Esilda. This Hans of Iceland, this brigand, paid by

the enemies of the Count without doubt has in his power papers whose loss compromises the days, already so detested of your father. I want to return these papers to him, along with his life.

ESILDA:

Ah! You don't know this Hans, this infernal brigand? Do you know he commands all the powers of darkness? Do you know how he topples mountains on villages. That his breath extinguishes lighthouses on the rocks? They've vainly tried to fight him; he's destroyed whole battalions. And do you expect, Ordener,.to alone resist this giant aided by the demon with your frail sword?

ORDENER:

And your prayers, Esilda, and the thought that I am fighting for you. Be sure of it, my Esilda, that they've much exaggerated to you the power and strength of this brigand. He's a man like any other, who deals out death until he receives it.

ESILDA:

If you die, friend—What do you want to become of me?

ORDENER:

Friend, if I remain here, what will become of your unfortunate father?

ESILDA:

My father! Go then, O my Ordener! And if you don't return, sorrow without hope kills; I shall have this tardy consolation. Friend, let this portrait of Esilda accompany you! May it be luckier than I am!

ORDENER:

It and your memory will never leave my heart.

(Ordener places a kiss on the young girl's face, then moves away to the left as Esilda moves away to the right.)

BLACKOUT/CURTAIN

ACT I
SCENE 3

The scene changes and represents the Morgue. Midnight strikes.

SPIAGUDRY:

(entering from the right with a book in one hand and a lamp in the other, reading)

"When a man lights his lamp death is with him before it may be put out." No offense to the wise doctor, it won't be thus with me tonight and I am going to put myself to bed.

A VOICE:

(off)

Spiagudry!

SPIAGUDRY:

(shivering)

What's that I hear!

VOICE:

Spiagudry.

SPIAGUDRY:

(Pointing to the room of corpses)

That voice is coming from there. Blessed Saint Hospice have pity on me.

(the door of the gate opens. A small man dressed in the skins of animals with a red and woolly beard and hair, armed with a large knife and an ax, comes from the room of corpses.)

HANS:

(speaking to Spiagudry, whose whole body trembles)

Do you know, old specter, that you've made me wait long enough? Do you wish by delaying me to exchange your bed of straw for one of those beds of stone? Well!

Is it that my presence is not agreeable to you?

SPIAGUDRY:

(bowing to the ground)

On the contrary, master. Can there exist for me a happiness greater than that of seeing Your Excellency?

HANS:

(in a somber tone)

Old fox! My Excellency orders you to reply. Do you know the name of the soldier who had the misfortune to be preferred by Gill Stadt—by this girl who is there beside him.

SPIAGUDRY:

Master, pardon, but I don't.

HANS:

(after roaring)

Well, by the ax of Ingolph, the leader of my race, I will exterminate all those wearing uniforms such as his. Perhaps the one on whom I wish vengeance will be found amongst the number. I have sworn it from the day Gill died and I've already given him a companion who must rejoice his cadaver.

(going to the gate and contemplating the remains of the young miner)

O my son! There you are without strength and without life; as cold as on the stone on which you lay, not long ago, just like your father choking a Norwegian bear in your arms.

You are no longer yourself, my blood. The unique hope of my race, the only link which attached me to this earth. Ah, if you had, like me, lived far from men, in the midst of forests, not hearing any other voices than those of the tempests, today I would not have to curse your weakness, to deplore your death and the fatal passion that this wretched creature ignited in your heart that led you to the tomb? Sad victim of a woman's caprice. You sought gold to enrich your mistress. You found death! Ah, bad luck to me who let you perish; bad luck to you, human race whose cowardly passions have caused the annihilation of the only being who weakened the hate I bear you. Tremble for my vengeance; it will be terrible. For my son will not inherit my stone ax. On the contrary, it's he who's going to bequeath to me his skull so as to drink from it hence forth, sea water, and men's blood.

(As he finishes these words, he removes the animal skin gloves and reveals his hands armed with claws like those of a wild beast, and seizing a dagger gets ready to enter the room of the dead.)

SPIAGUDRY:

(begging)

Just God, master: a dead man.

HANS:

Would you prefer that this blade sharpen itself on a living?

SPIAGUDRY:

How can Your Excellency thus profane— Your Lordship, Your Grace—

HANS:

Will you call it off, old living skeleton!

SPIAGUDRY:

By Saint Youssuf! By Saint Hospice!

HANS:

Don't speak of saints to the Devil! Leave me alone, I tell you!!

(He enters for a moment into the mortuary.)

SPIAGUDRY:

(yelling)

May Saint Waldemer have pity, not on my soul, but on my body!

HANS:

(reappearing and hiding something under his clothing)

There it is! My son, it's all which remains to me of you! Cursed thirst for gold. That's what ruined you.

SPIAGUDRY:

(in a wheedling tone)

Your Excellency's right. Gold itself is often purchased too dear.

HANS:

You make me think of it. Approach. Here's an iron box I found on that officer. It's firmly locked so it must contain gold. You will deliver it to the widow Stadt, in the Hamlet of Walbourg to pay her for her son. I think you are more cowardly than avaricious, and you will answer to me for this coffer.

SPIAGUDRY:

Oh, master, On my soul.

HANS:

Your soul? Not at all! On your flesh and on your bones.

(two great blows strike on the exterior door)

What's that? Doubtless, some dead man in a rush to come in?

SPIAGUDRY:

(all atremble)

No, master. They don't bring dead men after midnight.

(renewed knocking)

HANS:

Dead or living, he's hunting me. I am leaving by this skylight which allowed me to enter.

You, Spiagudry: be faithful and silent. The whole regiment of Munckolm will pass in review in your inn for cadavers. I swear it to you on Gill's skull.

(Hans disappears.)

ORDENER:

(outside)

Open on behalf of the Viceroy!

SPIAGUDRY:

(running to open the door, shouting.)

Ah, poor Spiagudry; you're done for!.

ORDENER:

(entering)

On honor, old geezer, I was beginning to believe it was the dead men lodged in this building who were in charge of opening the door.

SPIAGUDRY:

Pardon, lord; I was sleeping deeply.

ORDENER:

It seems to me that your dead don't sleep for it was doubtless they I heard just now distinctly arguing. Moreover, I didn't come here to busy myself about your affairs but to tell you about mine.

SPIAGUDRY:

Speak Lord, or rather take the trouble of coming into my laboratory.

ORDENER:

No, it's these cadavers that must detain us.

SPIAGUDRY:

(stupefied)

These cadavers! But Lord, you cannot see them.

ORDENER:

(tearing the lamp from the hand of Spiagudry and heading toward the room of the dead)

What! I cannot see the bodies which are there to be seen? Obey, willingly, geezer, or you will be forced to obey. Show me the clothes of Captain Dispolsen.

SPIAGUDRY:

Great Saint Youssouf have pity on me.

ORDENER:

(full of horror)

Just heaven! What an abominable profanation.

SPIAGUDRY:

Oh! Lord, mercy; it's not I (begging) if you knew. Did you see someone leave this building?

ORDENER:

Your accomplice, perhaps?

SPIAGUDRY:

(on his knees)

No, it's the guilty one; the only one who's guilty. I swear it even by this body so basely profaned.

ORDENER:

(in a much softer tone)

Old geezer, rise. And if you have not outraged the dead, at least don't shame old age. Who is the guilty one? Name him!

SPIAGUDRY:

In the name of heaven, lord. Don't speak so. From fear of—

ORDENER:

(half drawing his sword)

Fear won't make me shut up and it will make you speak.

SPIAGUDRY:

Well! The desecrator of this cadaver is the murderer of this officer. Notice the deep lacerations produced by the long sharp claws, on the body of this unfortunate. They name the murderer to you.

ORDENER:

What? Is it some wild animal? bear?

SPIAGUDRY:

No, my young lord.

ORDENER:

In that case, hasten to tell me his name.

SPIAGUDRY:

Well, it's—it's Hans of Iceland!

ORDENER:

Hans of Iceland! That execrable bandit!

SPIAGUDRY:

Don't call him bandit for he lives all alone.

ORDENER:

Since you know him so well, tell me where Hans of Iceland is hiding?

SPIAGUDRY:

He never hides; he simply wanders.

ORDENER:

If you are not his accomplice, you won't hesitate to escort me on his pursuit.

SPIAGUDRY:

You, noble lord, you? Full of youth, to run after certain death.

ORDENER:

Listen: this profanation of which I wish to believe you innocent exposes you to punishment for sacrilege. You must flee. I offer you my protection but on the condition that you lead me to the brigand's lair. Be my guide,

I will be your protector. If I reach Hans of Iceland, I will bring him here dead or alive. You can then prove your innocence. Here, meanwhile, more royal shillings than you can earn in a year.

SPIAGUDRY:

Thanks, master. But you won't forget I've done everything of which I am capable to dissuade you from your risky plan.

ORDENER:

So be it. I am counting on your honesty.

SPIAGUDRY:

Ah! Master, the word of Spiagudry is as pure as the gold you've just given him.

ORDENER:

May it not be otherwise. For I'll prove to you that the steel I wear is no less good than my gold. Let's leave.

SPIAGUDRY:

Let's leave.

(A groaning is heard. Spiagudry shivers.)

ORDENER:

Is there no other living inhabitant here but you?

SPIAGUDRY:

Ah, you remind me of my helper, Oglipiglap. A Lapplander who makes as much noise when he sleeps as an old woman waking up.

(At the moment Ordener and Spiagudry disappear, Hans of Iceland half opens the door of the dead and utters a second roar, addressing a threatening gesture to the young man and his guide.)

CURTAIN

ACT II
SCENE 4

The stage represents a deep valley; at the back a lake and wooded mountains.

AT RISE, dancers occupy the stage. A village celebration. Merchants of all sorts offer their wares to villagers who press around them. In the distance several young men, rivals in dexterity endeavor to hit with their muskets a bird placed at the top of a pole. Frederic and the Count D'Alefeld enter dressed as hunters.

FREDERIC:

(with an imperious air to Kennibol who is pulling a young village girl toward him.)

Well! What's this insolent soldier pretend?

KENNIBOL:

Softly, Mr. Officer. This young girl is my fiancée and I

won't suffer that after having made her dance for two long hours, against all propriety, you would still permit yourself to make her listen to things she mustn't hear, As for me, soldier for eight years, I forbid you, officer for eight days, to speak further to this young girl.

FREDERIC:

Wise guy! Do you know what you are laying yourself open to?

KENNIBOL:

Scarred soldier, I am here in the bosom of my family with the consent of my superiors and freed for the moment of all subjection to you. Moreover, like you I bear the heart of a man and a sword of steel.

FREDERIC:

I will chastise you.

COUNT D'ALEFELD:

(coming out of the crowd, seizing his son by the arm and dragging him downstage)

Imprudent one! What are you going to do? Did I make

you leave the Dungeon of Munckolm and order you to meet me in these parts for you to brawl with these soldiers?

(The ballet which was interrupted by the quarrel between Frederic and Kennibol now continues.)

Hear me, my son. What I have told you is of the greatest importance. It's time for you to know my position and the services I expect of you. The marriage of your sister with the son of the Viceroy no longer suffices to keep me in the Prince's favor if Harald is not completely overthrown. From the depths of his prison this former minister is still as formidable as in his palace. Already the King is cooling towards me. An intriguer named Dispolsen has obtained several secret audience. One doesn't know to what Harald aspires, but he doesn't just desire freedom, because a prisoner of state desires power. Necessarily he must die judicially. We must forge a crime we are preparing on him.

FREDERIC:

Much lower, father.

COUNT D'ALEFELD:

(rapidly)

Under pretext of inspecting the Northern provinces incognito I'm coming to provoke an insurrection that afterwards it will be easy for me to stifle. What worries me is the loss of several important papers relative to this plan, and that I have every reason to believe is in the power of Dispolsen.

FREDERIC:

Dispolsen! But lord, rumors ran yesterday that this officer had just been assassinated on the strand of Urchtal.

COUNT D'ALEFELD:

I know it, but no papers were found on him. Moreover, we will see. At this moment I am in pursuit of this famous Brigand, Hans of Iceland that I plan to put at the head of the revolt of the miners.

FREDERIC:

Order; I am ready to follow you.

COUNT D'ALEFELD:

I've given a rendezvous to several of my armed men on the other side of Lake Sparbo. Go, my son; put yourself at their head. As for me, I will stay in these parts where I hope to gather some information necessary to our projects. Keep close to the mountains; don't swerve from your route. Tomorrow, before daybreak, I will have rejoined you.

(Frederic moves away to the left and Alefeld goes back into the crowd.)

SPIAGUDRY:

(to Ordener who enters with him from the right)

This way, master! At last we've arrived at the place of this celebration which we've heard tell of for so long; still, I advise you not to stop here if we want to get closer to the village before this great black cloud breaks in water all over us.

(A Syndic enters dressed in black, preceded by a drummer; the dances cease, everybody groups around them. The Great Chancellor can be distinguished in the crowd.)

SYNDIC:

(reading in a loud voice)

"In the name of the king: Be it known to all the inhabitants of this province that:

"First, the head of Hans, native of Iceland, murderer and arsonist is placed at a price of 1000 royal crowns."

(lively murmurs from those present)

"Secondly: The head of Benignus Spiagudry, necromancer and blasphemer, former guardian of the morgue at Drontheim is placed at a price of four royal crowns!"

(bursts of laughter)

The head of these two men is offered to whoever will take it.

(terror by Spiagudry who vainly tries to drag away his master)

A YOUNG GIRL:

A price on the head of Hans! They'd do as well to put a price on the head of the devil; for they say that like him he has a cloven foot and the great wings of a bat.

KENNIBOL:

Who told you these stories, young girl? I myself observed this Hans of Iceland this morning in the gorges of Kole. He's a man like us, only he has the height of a forty-year-old poplar.

AN UNKNOWN:

(covered with a straw hat and rush mat)

Truly?

(Spiagudry shivers)

A VILLAGER:

Be he four or forty fathoms tall, I'm not the one who'll take it upon myself to go see him.

ALL:

Nor I! Nor I!

UNKNOWN:

Yet this one would be tempted to find Hans of Iceland

tomorrow in the ruins of Arbor, and the day after in the grotto of Waldborg.

ORDENER:

(excitedly)

Are you sure?

UNKNOWN:

(after having considered a moment and in a heavy voice)

Yes.

COUNT ALEFELD:

And how do you know him to be able to affirm it?

UNKNOWN:

I know where Hans of Iceland is just as I know where Benignus Spiagudry is. Neither the one nor the other is far from here at the moment.

SPIAGUDRY:

(trembling, low to Ordener)

Let's get out of here. Mercy, master, pity. Let's leave this cursed faubourg of hell!

(the storm that preceded the arrival of the unknown, breaks; lightning strikes breaking a tree not far from the group. Terrified, everyone disperses and disappears.)

CURTAIN

ACT II
SCENE 5

The scene changes and represents the interior of a rustic chamber of the most lugubrious appearance.

The back, opened in several places, allows rocks to be seen with a precipice and ravines. Side doors. That on the left is secured only by a flap of tapestry. Fire in the chimney. A table and chairs. Instruments of torture are placed here and there and at the back on the length of the wall. End of the storm.

BECHLIE:

(alone, seated by the fire, spinning)

What a terrible storm! One more like it and it will take to the depths of these caverns what it and its predecessors have spared of this tower cursed by heaven and men. But nine o'clock has just struck and Orugix hasn't come. What can be keeping him? They erected a gibbet at noon and it takes only six hours to come from Skougen to Wygla. Could he have had some extra work?

(noise outside)

At last, it's him!

(dryly)

Strangers! What are you coming here for? It wasn't men who indicated these ruins to you for shelter for all would have told you "Better the flare of the storm than the foyer of this cursed tower." Trust me, regain the road. And don't tell anybody that your faces have been lit by the lamp of the landlords of this place.

ORDENER:

Good woman. One would have to be mad to continue on his way in the midst of the precipices of these mountains after such weather.

BACHLIE:

Unfortunate: Don't rap on the sill of one who knows how to open no other door except that of the sepulcher.

ORDENER:

If the door of the sepulcher were indeed to open for me with yours, it shall not be said I have recoiled before a sinister word. My saber answers to me for everything. Come, take this gold.

BECHLIE:

(receiving the purse)

Gold! If it could guarantee the storms of heaven it would not escape the scorn of men. Well, stay then. I am going to prepare this room to receive you.

(she goes into the first hall to the right)

SPIAGUDRY:

May Saint Hospice protect us! You wished it, master. May we not have to repent of entering into this demon's oratory! Just God, master, a gibbet!

ORDENER:

Yes, and behold the saws of wood and iron, chains, iron collars; here's a wooden horse for torture and huge pincers.

SPIAGUDRY:

Great Saints of Paradise! Where are we?

ORDENER:

(continuing his inspection)

A roll of hemp cord, tongs, an ax.

SPIAGUDRY:

Then this is Hell's storehouse.

ORDENER:

Indeed. All this is strange and I begin to regret that my want of foresight has led you here.

SPIAGUDRY:

It's about time.

ORDENER:

Don't be terrified. No matter where you are, I am here with you.

SPIAGUDRY:

Much obliged.

ORDENER:

Are we not armed?

SPIAGUDRY:

Great defense! A saber of thirty inches against a gibbet of thirty cubits. Just heaven, master—

(raising the tapestry which closes one of the doors on the left)

Look there; at the back, on that heap of straw in the shadow.

ORDENER:

Well.

SPIAGUDRY:

Those motionless bodies. Three cadavers. Three hanged men, perhaps.

ORDENER:

Can't you see that they are young children sleeping on that pile of straw?

(someone raps violently on the outside door.)

BECHLIE:

(enters, followed by Hans disguised as a hermit, she opens)

Yet another stranger. No one can come in.

HANS:

(with a feigned sweetness that betrays his violence)

Woman, be silent. I will stay. Thunder enters without one's opening the door to him.

SPIAGUDRY:

(to Ordener, with terror)

Do you hear? Misfortune; misfortune to us!

HANS:

(with a benign, playful manner)

Accept me, worthy hostess, and God will bless you. You will grow old with your spouse, your children will grow up surrounded by the esteem of men, and they will be as their father was.

BECHLIE:

It's by remaining what we are that our children will grow old like us as the scorn of mankind, transmitted by our race from generation to generation.

ORDENER:

Then who are you? And what crimes are you guilty of?

BECHLIE:

What are you calling crimes? What do you call virtues? We enjoy a privilege here. The law commands us. We don't need virtues, nor do we commit crimes.

SPIAGUDRY:

The woman is mad.

BECHLIE:

(advancing on Spiagudry)

Mad! no. But since you wish it, learn where you are. I prefer to create horror than pity. I am not your mad woman but the wife of—

(a knocking at the door)

VOICE:

(outside, calling)

Bechlie!

BECHLIE:

(running to open)

It's his voice; it's finally him.

ORUGIX:

Oh! Oh! So many visitors! Woman, a storm may come and there will be a crowd sitting at our execrated table and sheltering under our cursed roof.

BECHLIE:

I was unable to prevent—

ORUGIX:

Eh! What's it matter. Gold is earned as well by nurturing a traveler as by strangling a bandit. Don't disturb yourselves, gentlemen. I thank you, brother hermit, for the benediction that, each morning at your passage over the hill, I see you give to my dwelling.

(examining him)

But in truth, up to now, you'd seemed very tall to me. And this very black beard had seemed white.

(Hans turns and laughs)

Hola! Bechlie! Serve us this quarter of lamb and put us to table. I'm hungry. I was delayed in the village of Burlock by that cursed Doctor Manryll who didn't want to give me more than twelve escalins per cadaver. They are giving forty to that old morgue guardian from Drontheim, may Hell confound him. Well, what's wrong with you gentlemen? Is it the wind which has thus pulled your wig over your face?

SPIAGUDRY:

(stuttering)

Yes, lord. The wind, the rain, the storm.

ORUGIX:

(laughing)

Come! Take heart, by Jove! And let's get acquainted; if your discourse proves as your appearance promises you must be amusing to hang.

(they sit at the table)

SPIAGUDRY:

(low and making horrible grimaces)

Thanks!

(aloud)

The master jokes—

ORIGIX:

Not at all. But wait, my guests, taste this beer, and sup

joyously, for such as you see me, I am a philosopher without a care. As for me, in my profession, just as happy as another man, My word, I laugh, I drink, I eat, I hang, and I sleep.

ORDENER:

(aside)

He kills and he sleeps. The unfortunate—

HANS:

How happy this wretch is!

ORUGIX:

Happy! Yes, brother hermit. See, the profession would be good if they didn't ruin it through the benefices. It's for that I'm especially angry with this damned guardian of the dead from Drontheim, what's his name already—Spluigry, Spagudry!

SPIAGUDRY:

(jumping in his seat.)

The Devil! Let's keep our incognito.

ORUGIX:

(to Spiagudry)

Tell me, my old doctor, couldn't you help me to discover the name of this sorcerer, your colleague? You don't reply. Has your wig made you deaf?

SPIAGUDRY:

No, master. I don't know this man and since he has the misfortune to displease you, I would surely be very annoyed to know him.

HANS:

As for me, I know him. His name is Benignus Spiagudry. He's tall, old, dry and bald.

(Spiagudry puts his hand on his wig)

He's got long hands like that of a thief who hasn't met a traveler in a week.

(Spiagudry hides his hands)

Bent back.

(Spiagudry stands erect)

OEUGIX:

Thanks father. I will recognize him and if his neck falls between my hands —

ORDENER:

But what wrongs have you to reproach him with?

ORUGIX:

His business resembles mine. He does all that he can to injure me. Would you believe that he has the impudence to dare to dispute with me the title to Hans of Iceland.

HANS:

(abruptly)

Hans of Iceland!

ORUGIX:

You know this famous brigand?

HANS:

Yes.

ORUGIX:

All brigands revert to the Hangman; isn't that true? What does this infernal Spiagudry do? He insists that they put a price on the head of Hans.

HANS:

(grinding his teeth)

He's the one who insisted on it?

ORUGIX:

Yes, I tell you. And it was solely so that the body would revert to him and that I may be frustrated, defrauded of my title.

HANS:

(with a diabolic laugh)

Now he is infamous!

ORUGIX:

But I will put this in order. Brother Hermit, the day Hans is hanged, come see me. We will sacrifice a fat pig in rejoicing

HANS:

Willingly. But do you know if I will be free on that particular day?

SPIAGUDRY:

(aside, examining him)

What a sound his voice has.

HANS:

(fixing Spiagudry in his turn)

Master Orugix, what is the torture for blasphemers, for mutilators of a corpse for example?

ORUGIX:

(emptying his glass with indifference.)

They used to bury him alive with the profaned cadaver.

HANS:

And now?

ORUGIX:

Oh! Now it's much softer.

SPIAGUDRY:

Much softer.

ORUGIX:

First they brand an "S" on the fat of his legs.

SPIAGUDRY:

(hiding his legs and breathing with difficulty)

And then?

ORUGIX:

They are satisfied with hanging him.

SPIAGUDRY:

Mercy. With hanging him.

ORUGIX:

What's with this old nut? He's looking at me with the air of a patient looking at the gallows.

HANS:

I see with pleasure they've returned to humanitarian principles.

(A great noise outside; general astonishment)

ORUGIX:

What a noise! Go see, Bechlie, what that can be.

BECHLIE:

(at the back)

It's a traveler in danger of perishing on the shores of the lake. A furious animal is pursuing him.

ORUGIX:

(after rising from the table.)

It's the bear from the ruins. The second scourge of the country!

HANS:

(aside, after having looked outside)

Friend. He has nothing to fear from them.

ALL:

Let's go to the aid of the unfortunate!

(They all leave except Spiagudry. Hans remains outside only for an instant. Soon he is seen to return in his usual costume, dressed in skins with his ax. Hans places himself behind Spiagudry and makes threatening gestures towards him during the following monologue.)

SPIAGUDRY:

(Hans at the back)

Yes, run, run. If not for the fear of being rejoined later I would run, too. But in a different direction. I'm thinking about it. If in their absence I were to busy myself breaking the envelop of iron that contains my riches. For I consider this coffer as belonging to me, the spoils of the dead, my pensioners reverting to me by law. Moreover a thief who steals from another makes the Devil laugh over it. And if someone tempted by the four royal shillings recognized me and arrested me, with the aid of this treasure I would buy myself off. So this lucky casket won't escape me.

(At the moment Spiagudry sits on the ground and armed with a hammer prepares to break the lock on the coffer, the redoubtable Hans finds himself before him.)

SPIAGUDRY:

(frozen)

Ah! Just heaven! Who've I seen!

HANS:

It's I. This casket will save you, you say?

(he laughs, then adds in a somber tone)

Spiagudry, is this the way to Walbourg?

SPIAGUDRY:

Walbourg? Lord, master—I was going there.

HANS:

(in a thunderous voice)

You were going to Walbourg! You were leading an enemy to me! Thanks! There will be one less among the living. Listen; you've betrayed me.

SPIAGUDRY:

No, Your Grace, no Excellency.

HANS:

(fixing him with devouring eyes)

You'd like to deceive me again. No longer hope to do it. I was on the roof of the morgue when you sealed your pact with that senseless young man. It was my voice and step you heard. It was I you saw only for an instant. It was I!

SPIAGUDRY:

Mercy!

HANS:

(with a horrible laugh)

Rather ask your salvation from this coffer which you were expecting just now.

SPIAGUDRY:

My sweet master!

HANS:

I advised you to be faithful and silent. You were unable to be faithful; in the future you will have to be silent.

SPIAGUDRY:

(half dead)

Mercy! Mercy!

HANS:

Don't be afraid. I won't separate you from your treasure. Don't be desolate about leaving your young companion without a guide. I promise you he will go where you are going. You will only show him the way. Come on!

(Hans seizes the poor concierge with his iron hand and drags him to the rocks from where he hurls him into the lake.)

ORDENER:

(reappearing)

What death cry is making itself heard? Spiagudry! Ah, poor unfortunate; it's I who have caused his ruin.

(Hans moves away after having uttered a roar of satisfaction. Orugix, Bechlie, and some peasants attracted by the screams of Spiagudry arrive and stop frozen with terror)

CURTAIN

ACT III
SCENE 6

The stage represents the interior of the ruins of Arbor. It's a dark and deep gallery. It terminates abruptly three quarters the length of the stage with some stone steps which seem to have once belonged to a stairway that a landslide has left suspended above a precipice.

HANS:

(alone. He appears leaning towards an object at the left behind the rubbish and cannot be seen. With a strange look on his lips he seems at length to savor its features. Finally, he cries out.)

They're walking in the gallery! Would it be the Chancellor of the two kingdoms already?

(bursts of laughter)

No. It's not a man, but it's still an enemy. It's a wolf. His eyes shine, he's famished and the odor of cadavers attracts him. As for him, he will soon attract other famished wolves. Be welcome wolf of Smiasen. You are so old they say you cannot die. They won't say that tomorrow.

(he rushes on the wolf that appears art the right, clasps it firmly and hurls it to the ground, dead, strangled. A white and shaggy mass that one notices amongst the rubble rises and stirs about. It's a bear. The man shouts with a roar and gives it a kick.)

Friend! Who called you? Go away!

(The bear retires to the left where the man was first.)

There you are dead, terrible wolf. Indeed, you devoured stray travelers, but you are dead in your turn. You will never eat any more men; that's a shame.

(hearing a slight noise at the left he shouts)

Friend! Ah! Miserable Friend! Here, come here.

(pointing to the body of the wolf)

Here's your prey. Leave me alone with mine.

(the bear smells the wolf and shakes its head in discontent)

I understand. This one's already too dead for you. You are refined in your pleasures, Friend, as much as a man. You want your nourishment to be alive until the moment you tear it apart. You only enjoy that which is suffering. We resemble each other for I am not a man. I am above that wretched species. I am a ferocious beast like you.

(caressing the bear)

I wish that you could speak, companion, Friend, to tell me if it equals my joy— the joy which palpitates in your bear's entrails when you devour the entrails of a man. But no, I don't wish to hear you speak for fear your voice would recall the human voice to me.

(the bear rolls on the ground as if striving to please its master)

Yes, growl at my feet, I love your raucous cries and your shaggy mug. They frighten men. Like me, you have white teeth. Still, it's not our fault if they are not as red as a new wound.

(Noise outside, Hans gets up from the stone on which

he is seated.)

Rise up, Friend. Here now is a man. When one speaks of Hell, Satan shows his hoof. Companion Friend leave me alone for a moment. Hey, outside.

(The monster obeys and rushes toward the exterior steps of the gallery and descends backwards with the aid of shrubs with which the ruins are strewn, disappearing over the precipice. The Grand Chancellor wrapped in a cloak enters by the left.)

HANS:

Stranger: be Unwelcome.

(Count D'Alefeld shivers but soon gets hold of himself; he stops and examines Hans, who adds)

You won't have a breath of a voice to boast of having seen me.

COUNT D'ALEFELD:

Listen, I don't come as an enemy, but as a friend. My intention is to do you a service if you are the one I seek.

HANS:

Meaning to exact a service from me. You waste your steps. I don't render any services, except to those who are tired of life.

COUNT D'ALEFELD:

By your words, I indeed recognize you for the one I need. But your height? Hans of Iceland is a giant. That cannot be you.

HANS:

Add my renown to my height and you will see me taller than this rock.

COUNT D'ALEFELD:

In that case, as I was saying, it is your sole interest that leads me here.

HANS:

Are you coming to give me advise as to some well to poison? Some village to burn, or some Musketeer of Munckolm to strangle?

COUNT D'ALEFELD:

Perhaps. Listen The miners of Norway are revolting. Do you know how many disasters this can lead to?

HANS:

Yes. Murder, Arson, Pillage.

COUNT D'ALEFELD:

I offer you all that.

HANS:

(with a burst of laughter)

To take it, I have no need for you to offer me.

COUNT D'ALEFELD:

In the name of the miners, I propose to you command of the insurrection.

(hurling a purse)

Here are the benefices of your command.

HANS:

(rejecting the purse with his foot.)

I don't want it. If I wanted your gold or your blood I wouldn't wait for your permission to satisfy myself.

COUNT D'ALEFELD:

Reflect before refusing my offers.

HANS:

Chancellor of Norway, no!

COUNT D'ALEFELD:

(recoiling)

Who told you—?

HANS:

(grasping him by the arm)

Minister of Norway, if our two souls were speeding towards heaven at this moment I think that Satan would hesitate before deciding which of the two is the brigand.

COUNT D'ALEFELD:

(after having rested his hand on the guard of his sword)

At least, if you deliver to me a box found on the shores of the Urchtal, you could expect all my gratitude.

HANS:

(as if remembering)

Ah! Then that box is of great importance?

COUNT D'ALEFELD:

Yes.

HANS:

Well! You shan't have it.

COUNT D'ALEFELD:

I will assure you an immense fortune; I will ask your pardon of the King.

HANS:

Rather ask me yours. Hear me, Count D'Alefeld. Tigers

don't feed on hyenas. I am going to let you leave my presence alive because you are a bad one. And each moment of your life, each thought of your soul engenders misfortune for men and a crime for you. As for your officer, it's not for me to appropriate to myself the box that you want. Though I murdered him, it was his uniform that condemned him, like this other wretch that you see here.

(As he finishes these words, Hans of Iceland drags the minister towards an object hidden in the shadows.)

COUNT D'ALEFELD:

(with a terrifying scream)

Heavens! Frederic! My son!

HANS:

(with a burst of atrocious laughter)

You can yell, Count, but you can't revive him.

COUNT D'ALEFELD:

(leaning over the body of his son)

Frederic—

HANS:

(in a more somber voice)

Weep for your son. As for me, I am avenging mine.

COUNT D'ALEFELD:

(rising suddenly and drawing his sword)

Help! Vengeance! Vengeance!

(at the Count's shouts three men, sabers in hand, rush into the gallery)

COUNT D'ALEFELD:

Death to this brigand! Death to the murderer of my son!

(Hans of Iceland, surprised by such an abrupt attack, has seized his ax and for a few moments makes headway against his enemies, but soon, pressed by numbers he is forced to beat a retreat. At last he is on the steps of the stairs suspended over the abyss.)

COUNT D'ALEFELD:

Fine, my friends. Let's push the monster off this precipice.

HANS:

Before I fall in the stars will fall in.

COUNT D'ALEFELD:

Wretch! You've committed your last crime. Courage, my friends!

(Hans, still fighting with his right hand pulls a little trumpet that hangs from his belt, and makes a prolonged, raucous noise on it. A few seconds later the bear appears at the broken end of the stairs and presents his sharp jaws to the enemies of his master. Hans, profiting by this aid, rushes on the aggressors and puts them to flight.)

HANS:

Thanks my brave Friend

(he lets a scorching outburst of laughter be heard.)

CURTAIN

ACT III
SCENE 7

The stage represents the grotto of Valderhog. It is hollowed in the rock and lighted only at the back through some crevices which only allow the sky and distant mountains to be seen, In the midst of the cavern, slightly to the left is a stone Druid altar surrounded by human bones.

ORDENER:

(arriving by one of the bends on the left, after having cast his eyes around)

No one! In vain have I sounded all the turnings of this vast grotto. I've been unable to meet the object of my search. Why can't I meet this Hans of Iceland? Darling Esilda! Must I renounce the hope of returning your unlucky father to you?

(he leans on the druid altar.)

VOICE:

Young man! It's with feet touching the sepulcher that you came to this place.

(At this moment the head of Hans of Iceland is revealed on the other side of the stone altar with his ferocious smile.)

ORDENER:

(unmoved)

And with a hand touching his sword.

HANS:

(armed with his ax and revealing himself completely)

It's I!

ORDENER:

It's I.

HANS:

I was expecting you.

ORDENER:

And as for me, I was doing better; I was searching for you.

HANS:

(crossing his arms on his breast)

Do you know who I am?

ORDENER:

Yes.

HANS:

And you haven't any fear?

ORDENER:

None any more.

HANS:

(smiling)

Then you experienced fear coming here.

ORDENER:

That of not meeting you.

HANS:

You brave me, and your feet have just stumbled over human cadavers!

ORDENER:

Perhaps tomorrow they will stumble on yours!

HANS:

(with a shiver of rage)

Take care, I am going to rush you.

ORDENER:

I am waiting for you.

HANS:

You teach me what pity is.

ORDENER:

And me what scorn is.

HANS:

Child, what death do you want from me?

ORDENER:

Yours.

(Hans starts to laugh)

Listen, you know Count D'Alefeld who paid you to take an iron coffer from an officer you murdered on the shores of Urchtal?

HANS:

D'Alefeld! Wait, yes, I know him; yesterday I drank his son's blood from the skull of mine.

ORDENER:

Your sight weighs on me. We've got to finish this. You stole an iron box from an officer of Munckolm?

HANS:

(shivering at this word)

Munckolm! And as for you, would you also be an

officer of Munckolm?

ORDENER:

No.

HANS:

(sadly)

So much the worse.

ORDENER:

Listen: where is this box you stole from your victim?

HANS:

By my ax! Now there's a box that really troubles many wits!

ORDENER:

Is it in the power of Count D'Alefeld?

HANS:

(smiling)

No.

ORDENER:

You lie, for you are laughing.

HANS:

Believe what you like.

ORDENER:

(in a thundering voice)

You must give it to me, this box!

HANS:

Is it to me that you dare give orders?

ORDENER:

I will give them to the Demon in Hell.

HANS:

(grasping his ax)

You'll soon be able to do that. It was only up to me to break your bones and drink your blood when you got here, but I was curious to see the perky sparrow rush on the vulture.

ORDENER:

Wretch! Defend yourself.

HANS:

First time anyone's said that to me.

(unable to contain himself, he rushes roaring on the Druid altar. Ordener turning this way and that, studies the movements of the enemy he wishes to strike. Finally, the terrible Hans utters a horrifying scream, his ax entangled in the folds of the young man's cloak which he's used as a shield. Ordener escapes him.)

ORDENER:

(resting his sword blade on the breast of the disarmed monster)

Deliver to me the box of iron that you stole in such a cowardly way!

HANS:

No.

ORDENER:

Consider, wretch.

HANS:

No, and be damned,

ORDENER:

In that case take up your ax so we can continue.

HANS:

(with a disdainful look)

Child, you act generous, as if I had need of it.

(with a leap Hans of Iceland is ten feet from him and seizing an enormous rock hurls it at his adversary who succeeds in avoiding this blow. Hans now has retaken his ax and the combat renews sharply. But soon luck is not equal. Ordener's weapon breaks in his hand as it meets that of his enemy. Already the monster is ready to seize his prey; his arm is going to strike.)

HANS:

(with strength)

Have you something to say to God or the Devil before dying?

ORDENER:

(pressing her portrait against his lips)

Darling Esilda, goodbye!

(Suddenly the sound of a horn, then a distant roaring is heard outside. The brigand stops, the noise increases; the clamors of men are mixed with the plaintive groans of a bear that is seen crossing the rocks swiftly pursued by hunters. Several rifle shots are heard.)

HANS:

Friend, Friend, I am coming to help you. Here I am!

(Hans disappears through one of the crevices at the back leaving Ordener free.)

ORDENER:

(alone) O fury!

I am without arms! He's escaping me. Unlucky Harald.

(leaves on the track of Hans.)

CURTAIN

ACT III
SCENE 8

The stage represents a public square in Drontheim. To the right one of the exterior doors of The Palace of Justice. In the back is a stake bearing some inscription. A large number of the inhabitants of Drontheim reach the palace of Justice from different sides and stop. They are sad and in consternation. Noticeable among the matrons are Maase and Olly. Also present, the young soldier Kenniibol with his arm in a sling.

OLLY:

In a few moments the former Grand Chancellor of Norway, the benefactor of the people shall have ceased to live.

MAASE:

On the big square, the scaffold is hung in black. And from here I observe the Executioner in great red dress, his cutlass in hand awaiting his victim.

OLLY:

Noble Count, virtuous Harald, vainly do they proclaim you as the leader of this unfortunate insurrection of miners. Everybody refuses to believe you are the author of that crime; and yet you are going to bear the punishment. May your unjustly spilled blood pour back over the heads of your judges.

KENNIBOL:

Yes, and on the monstrous Icelander who, during the bloody encounter of rebels and royal troops in the gorges of Kole, wiped out both parties under enormous fragments of rocks that he rained down on them. More than one third of my regiment remains in those somber defiles, and myself —

MAASE:

Let the truly guilty ones perish! Justice for the innocent.

(Four o'clock strikes)

ORDENER:

(arriving precipitously, completely defeated)

Just heavens! My friends, what's going on here? What are these deadly preparations for? What's become of Harald? His daughter? Speak!

(before any of those present is able to respond to these questions, the door of the palace of justice opens and a detachment of soldiers in the midst of which is found Count Harald being escorted to his death—slowly enters. Harald walks with a calm expression, observing the crowd. D'Alefeld in costume of a great judge comes next. At this sight Ordener becomes petrified. Suddenly, from the wings, Esilda's voice cries out.)

ESILDA:

Let me go! Let me go!

(at the same moment the disheveled young girl, clothes in disorder runs out and falls in the arms of her father who presses her to his heart.)

HARALD:

My daughter.

ESILDA:

My father.

(the funeral cortege stops. Bursts of tears on all sides)

D'ALEFELD:

(coldly coming forward)

Let them take this young girl away.

ESILDA:

No, no. By all that you hold most dear: grant me the mercy of dying with him.

D'ALEFELD:

(coldly)

Let them be separated.

ORDENER:

Barbarian, do more! Without pity for the despair of this young girl have her thrown into the darkest of your dungeons. Let her expire for the crime of having wanted to embrace her father as he marched to undeserved death. This act of justice is yet more worthy of you.

HARALD:

Halt, imprudent youth! Let my ruin, at least, not entail yours. Esilda, we must leave each other forever. But alone, without support in this world, what will become of you?

ORDENER:

God and Ordener will watch over the poor orphan. Noble Count, will you grant me Esilda for a spouse?

HARALD:

Brave young man! The daughter of the condemned is yours! Your name?

ORDENER:

(revealing his chest)

Ordener Guldenlen, son of the Viceroy of Norway.

(everyone uncovers)

D'ALEFELD:

(removing his hat)

The son of the Viceroy? My daughter's fiancée?

ORDENER:

Himself.

D'ALEFELD:

(no longer able to contain himself)

Let the sentence be executed.

HARALD:

Now I can die.

ESILDA:

Father!

D'ALEFELD:

Soldiers, obey.

(Esilda faints on the breast of her father and is delivered by him to the hands of Ordener. The unfortunate Harald leaves in the midst of the guards, as he appears to call down the benediction of heaven on the children. The people follow him.)

ORDENER:

And I cannot do anything to prevent the execution of this fatal judgment!

(Esilda, still unconscious, is carried to a stone bench by Ordener and old Olly and Maase who've approached to freely give their assistance. Hans of Iceland dressed in a beaten down hat and covered by a straw matt comes in and strikes Ordener on the shoulder.)

HANS:

Brave youth, do you recognize me?

ORDENER:

Monster. I've finally found you again; it's heaven that sends you!

HANS:

No, it's Hell. Thank it for this meeting and especially that of your faithful guide Spiagudry who's returning for a while to his former dwelling.

(at this moment two men bearing on a litter an object covered with a black flag cross the back of the stage.

Hans makes a sign for them to stop.)

HANS:

It's he who is going to deliver to you this coffer to which you attach so high a price.

ORDENER:

(excitedly)

The iron coffer. Speak. Where is it?

HANS:

(raising the cover of the litter)

Heavens, look rather.

(the porters and the litter move away)

ORDENER:

(receiving the coffer)

The box. But O heaven, how to open it?

HANS:

(tearing it from his hands)

Child. Give it to me.

(Hans breaks open the box and delivers to Ordener the papers it contains.)

ORDENER:

Poor Esilda! May I get there in time.

(runs off shouting)

Stop! Stop!

HANS:

(at the back of the stage)

Will this young madman succeed in depriving the scaffold of its prey? By Ingolph! It won't be in vain that the executioner shall have erected it.

(He runs out on the trail of Ordener. Great murmur outside, shouting.)

VOICES SHOUTING:

Long Live Harald!

ESILDA:

(coming to)

Where am I? What horrible dream have I had? My Father. Great God—Where is my father?

HARALD:

(arriving precipitously followed by Ordener and the people)

Near you, my cherished Esilda; and here's my liberator. At his voice, despite D'Alefeld, the people snatched me from my executioners. These papers prove my innocence.

PEOPLE:

Long live Harald! Long Live Ordener!

(Ordener and Esilda are in each others arms)

(Kennibol rushes in; a great tumult is heard)

ORDENER:

What an uproar!

KENNIBOL:

Milords, Count D'Alefeld is no more. Hardly had you disappeared when a little man or rather a demon incarnate broke through the crowd and advancing toward the judges platform balancing their president in the air. He shouted, "Companions, you won't be deprived of the pleasure of seeing a man die. An innocent man was going to perish; a great criminal is going to replace him."

He spoke and with a leap he was on the scaffold, the executioner's chopper in hand and the Count of D'Alefeld died.

(The uproar is now at its height)

VOICES OFF:

Hans of Iceland. Death to Hans of Iceland.

(The people flee full of terror. Harald and Elisa withdraw into the palace of Justice. Ordener follows them. Then Hans of Iceland arrives pursued by Munkcholm's Musketeers. He rushes to the stake, tears it down and uses it like a club. Soon hit by a musket shot the monster falls to the ground shouting with rage.)

HANS:

Death and Furies! I am beaten.

CURTAIN

ACT III
SCENE 9

The stage is divided in two. To the left the interior of a dark dungeon with an iron door placed between the wings. The other part represents a guard house lit only by a lamp placed on the party wall. Door at the back.

KENNIBOL:

(and several soldiers in the guard house.)

Come on, my friends: long live joy. Hans of Iceland, over whom we have to watch tonight, is there in the neighboring cell. Well chained and no longer in a condition to injure us any more. Let's drink to his happy hanging which must take place tomorrow at daybreak.

SOLDIER:

(gaily)

To his happy hanging!

(Hans rises on the stone bench on which he was sleeping near the shared wall.)

HANS:

Musketeers of Munckholm!

(roaring he tries to break his chains)

Hell! So near me, and unable to annihilate them!

(rattles his chains)

JAILOR:

What's that uproar? What do you want?

HANS:

I'm cold. My stone bed is hard and wet. Bring me a bed of straw so as to sleep.

JAILOR:

I'm going to bring you what you ask. Do you have any money?

HANS:

No.

JAILOR:

What? Not some gold Ducats?

HANS:

No.

JAILOR:

Some little royal shillings?

HANS:

No, I tell you.

JAILOR:

Some poor six pennies?

HANS:

No! Nothing with which to purchase the skin of a rat or the soul of a man.

JAILOR:

That's different. In that case, you are wrong to complain. Your cell isn't as cold as that you'll be sleeping in tomorrow, without, I swear to you, noticing the hardness of the bed.

(starting to leave)

ORUGIX:

(entering)

Mr. Hans, I am Orugix, the Executioner, and tomorrow I must have the honor of hanging Your Excellency on this pretty new gibbet in Drontheim Square.

HANS:

Well, and so what?

ORUGIX:

After your death your body belongs to me by law; still the law gives you the option to sell it to me. In conscience, how much do you want for it?

Now for the two of us.

HANS:

One moment. First give me what I asked of you.

JAILOR:

(leaving)

That's fair.

HANS:

(to Orugix who is counting on his fingers)

Are you calculating already what you are going to earn off my carcass?

ORUGIX:

Yes. Don't you belong to me?

HANS:

When day appears you will come seek it.

JAILOR:

Here's your hay.

HANS:

Here's your gold.

ORUGIX:

Till tomorrow.

HANS:

(with a terrifying laugh)

Till tomorrow.

(Orugix and the Jailor leave)

KENNIBOL:

(in the guard room to his half drunk comrades) Now comrades, if you will. To wake you up and drive from our brains the heavy vapors of this liquor, I'm going to sing you a song I've just composed.

SOLDIERS:

Yes! yes! yes!

KENNIBOL:

(singing)

Do you know this famous brigand?

This celebrated Hans of Iceland?

This wild, ferocious monster?

Hidden in the shape of a man.

Travelers stretch your legs

Flee and beware his rage

No rest in these parts.

Don't sleep, don't sleep.

CHORUS OF SOLDIERS:

Don't sleep.

(Hans approaches the wall and listens with an attentive ear.)

KENNIBOL:

(singing)

But the brigand finally succumbed

Travelers resume your courage.

He's fallen beneath our blows

His fall's the work of Munckolm Musketeers.

Tomorrow he takes a leap

So till tomorrow we must drink

Friends, let's drink to our glory

Don't sleep! Don't sleep!

CHORUS OF SOLDIERS:

(succumbing to sleep)

Don't sleep!

HANS:

They are singing their victory! They brave me, these execrable soldiers. And I cannot overturn this wall on them, and I cannot break these irons that restrain me! Spirit of Ingolph reanimate my strength and my furor. Allow me to exterminate the last of these Musketeerrs of Munckolm to satisfy the shade of my son!

KENNIBOL:

Bravo! It seems my song has produced its usual effect. You're already snoring like the organ of the Cathedral of Drontheim. This Hans of Iceland, the Devil take his soul, has given us, as they say, a good deal of trouble. But, still, he's captured, and we can really close our eyes for a moment until he twists on a certain rope, that Master Orugix, the cleverest maker of slipknots in all Norway will soon present him with.

(Kennibol falls asleep on a table by his comrades. At this moment, Hans of Iceland, who has not ceased his fearful struggles to break his chains, utters a cry of joy. He's succeeded in shaking loose the stone in which his chain is fixed. He cocks his ear for a moment, and hearing nothing in the soldiers' room makes new efforts and succeeds in tearing the loosened stone from the wall. But the fall of the block makes Kennibol shiver, and half asleep he starts humming the refrain of his song.)

KENNIBOL:

Don't sleep!

(Now Hans of Iceland manages to pass his arm through the opening he's just made and lights some straw from the lamp burning on the soldier's table.)

HANS:

(with a roar of joy)

O Gill! O my son. You are going to be avenged. Let all who bear the name Munckolm perish!

(Hardly uttering these words, gathering his straw he sets it alight in a way to consume his prison. The back and left side of the prison room are constructed of timber. The flames make rapid progress. Soon the whole edifice is on fire; the support joints consumed detach and fall on every side. The soldiers flee towards the wall at the back which has just caved in with tumult. Finally, Hans of Iceland, seeming like the genius of destruction has not ceased to further the progress of the fire; wishing to flee in his turn he finds himself suddenly stopped by a crowd of armed men who aim at him with their muskets and force him to return on his tracks. The monster seeing no other place of safety for himself rushes towards one of the sides of the building that the flames have not yet reached. At first he seems to brave his enemies when suddenly the beam to which he's attached collapses under him and drags him into a furnace into which he disappears amidst a vortex of flames. The people let out a great yell of joy to which there is a horrible roaring in response coming from the place where Hans of Iceland was seen to disappear.)

CURTAIN

ABOUT THE AUTHOR

Frank J. Morlock has written and translated many plays since retiring from the legal profession in 1992. His translations have also appeared on Project Gutenberg, the Alexandre Dumas Père web page, Literature in the Age of Napoléon, Infinite Artistries.com, and Munsey's (formerly Blackmask). In 2006 he received an award from the North American Jules Verne Society for his translations of Verne's plays. He lives and works in México.

www.ingramcontent.com/pod-product-compliance
Lightning Source LLC
LaVergne TN
LVHW041628070426
835507LV00008B/507